Jennifer
With love,
Daddy & Mommy
Easter 1985

TEACH ME
HOW TO PRAY!

Teach Me How to Pray!

101 PRAYER-POEMS

BY

MARY DIXON THAYER

ILLUSTRATED
BY
KAREN HELLYER

CHRISTIANICA CENTER
6 NORTH MICHIGAN AVENUE
CHICAGO ILLINOIS 60602

International Standard Book Number: 0-911346-08-2

Illustrations © 1984
Christianica Center
All Rights Reserved

Original Title: The Child on His Knees
Copyright, 1926
by The Macmillan Company
All Rights Reserved

This edition is reprinted by arrangement with
Macmillan Publishing Company,
a division of Macmillan, Inc.

Manufactured in the United States of America

1 2 3 4 5 6 7 90 89 88 87 86 85 84

ILLUSTRATIONS

And I know I am not
Kneeling here alone! 15

Dear God, I know a little path
All covered soft and deep 23

Lovely Lady dressed in blue—
Teach me how to pray 31

I know wherever I may be
That God is looking down at me 43

Dear God, why do you care so much
If I am good or bad? 55

O God, I've learned such lovely things
About you from a rose! 67

I like to think the days are steps
On which you've set my feet 79

Why are some people sick, dear God,
And hungry and afraid? 91

I wish I'd been a child, dear God,
When you were little too! 103

Instead of lying there and thinking
How comfy beds can be 119

*For all children, everywhere,
but especially for Molly.*

PRAYER-POEMS

After Communion	41
Afterwards	28
Angels	112
Answer, The	56
At Night	80
At Play	38
Autumn Prayer	22
Being Taught	45
Comfort	97
Coming Back	69
Difference, The	100
Different Ways	118
Do You Really	36
Early Prayer	17
Excuses	114
Finding You	37
First Communion	40
First Present, The	93
Follow the Leader	125
For You	75
Forgetting	60
Forgive Me	56
Gift, A	104

Giving Back	47
Good Way, A	108
Growing	99
Hopes	45
How Kind!	71
How Nice!	82
How to Turn Fun into Prayers	124
I Know	48
I Love You	50
I Think	72
If	85
If I Should Die	73
If I Were You	107
If Only	102
In Church	14
In the Morning	29
Invitation, An	39
Just Think	52
Knowing	42
Late Prayer	18
Learning	44
Little Prayer, The	13
Lonely Feeling, The	68
Lovely Lady Dressed in Blue	30
Loving	76
Main Thing, The	70

Maybe	110
Messages	62
Mistake, The	96
Not Unless	113
Now	86
O Do!	47
Of Course	57
People	105
Perhaps	58
Perhaps He Won't	46
Plans	49
Please!	64
Prayer for Sad Times	16
Presents	92
Puzzle, A	111
Remembering	127
Remind Me	117
So Much!	95
Some Children	87
Some Days	94
Sometimes	74
Spring Prayer	19
Stairs, The	78
Summer Prayer	20
Suppose	126
Surest Way, The	127

Take All of Me	114
Tell Me What?	116
Thanksgiving	33
Thing to Do, The	49
Thinking	59
Thought, A	77
Thoughts	84
To the Blessed Mother	81
To Think!	89
Trading	122
Trying	98
Very Time, The	109
Waiting	115
Waking Up	106
What I Do Know	90
What to Do	122
What Will I Do?	88
When I'm Old	83
When You Were Little	51
Why Do You Care?	54
Winter Prayer	26
Wish, A	27
Wishing	39
Words	65
Wrong Idea	123
Your Friends	121

TEACH ME
HOW TO PRAY!

BY MARY DIXON THAYER

THE LITTLE PRAYER

Some of the prayers I ought to know
    Have words that are so long
I can't remember what they are,
    Or where they all belong.

And then I feel like crying, God,
    For I suppose I should
Know all those prayers by heart—and
        O!
    I *do* want to be good!

But mother says you understand
    That I am very small,
And that you like it if I pray
    In my own words and all . . .

Now, when I can't remember how
    A prayer is supposed to go—
I kneel down anyway and say
    "Dear God, I love you so!"

Teach Me How to Pray!

IN CHURCH

O! Here I am, dear God,
    Kneeling at your throne,
And I know I am not
    Kneeling here alone!

For I know that angels
    All around must be,
With their white wings folded,
    And their eyes on me.

Yes! There is an angel
    Always in this place,
Kneeling at your altar
    And hiding his face . . .

God, I know that you are
    Here because of me,
And I feel your nearness,
    Though I cannot see . . .

*And I know I am not
   Kneeling here alone!*

TEACH ME HOW TO PRAY!

And I kneel and whisper
    "God! I love you so!"
And the angels pass me
    Softly, tippy-toe . . .

A PRAYER FOR SAD TIMES

Do anything you want with me,
    Dear God, for I don't care
So long as you will let me love
    You always, everywhere!

Do anything you want with me,
    Dear God, for it is true
That everything you do is done
    To bring me nearer you!

BY MARY DIXON THAYER

EARLY PRAYER

God, please make me good today
   When I work and when I play!

It is easy, God, you see,
   For a little child like me

To forget you always know
   What I think, and where I go,

How I act, and that you're sad
   Every single time I'm bad!

O! Please make me good today
   When I work and when I play!

Teach Me How to Pray!

LATE PRAYER

Dear God! How beautiful are all
   The stars! I know that they would fall

Unless you kept them where they are.
   I know, dear God, that every star

Goes only where you tell it to,
   And does what it is meant to do.

O! When I look up at the sky,
   Sometimes it almost makes me cry

To think that even stars obey
   You better than I do each day!

BY MARY DIXON THAYER

SPRING PRAYER

What do you think, dear God?
    Down in the woods I found
  A flower dressed in blue
    Coming out of the ground!

What do you think, dear God?
    Today I saw a tree
  All full of baby leaves
    Shaking their heads at me!

What do you think, dear God?
    I picked a buttercup!
  And underneath my feet
    A little star looked up!

O! Thank you, God, for all
    This lovely time of year!
  Thank you for everything
    That you have done down here!

Teach Me How to Pray!

SUMMER PRAYER

What fun it is to be a child
    Upon a summer's day!
  O God, you know what fun it is
    To be a child and play!

The sky is a blue china bowl,
    And in it the clouds float,
  And one is like a big white swan
    With a long, curly throat!

And one is like an old, old man
    With a gray beard, and there
  Is one just like a lady with
    A scarf around her hair!

O God! What fun it is to lie
    Upon a hill and look
  At pictures in the sky, instead
    Of only in a book!

BY MARY DIXON THAYER

O God! What fun it is to hear
    The daisies talking to
The wind, as he comes running by,
    And says "how do you do?" . . .

Teach Me How to Pray!

AUTUMN PRAYER

The leaves are dressed in red and gold,
    And they come floating far . . .
They look like fairies—and I think
    Perhaps some of them are!

Dear God, I know a little path
    All covered soft and deep
With fairies—dressed in red and gold—
    All fallen fast asleep!

I know a place where angels come,
    With folded wings, to pray . . .
At least, I think they do—I think
    I saw one there today!

At any rate, dear God, it is
    The sort of place, you know,
That angels would be in if they
    Could choose where they would go.

Dear God, I know a little path
All covered soft and deep

TEACH ME HOW TO PRAY!

I like to run down there and say
    My prayers, dear God! I kneel
Upon the ground, and look around,
    And then I seem to feel

The angels moving softly on
    The grass, and trees lean down,
And whisper "Say a prayer for us!"
    Sometimes they put their brown

Arms gently round me, whispering
    "O pray for us—O pray!"
And so I do, dear God, you know
    The prayer for trees I say—

The one that asks you please to give
    Them lots of birds to sing
Among their branches, and a lot
    Of new leaves in the spring . . .

BY MARY DIXON THAYER

And snow to keep them warm when their
    Bare legs begin to freeze,
And all the rain they want, dear God!
    That is my prayer for trees.

WINTER PRAYER

The world is covered up with snow
   Today, dear God! I want to go

And play in it before the sun
   Comes out and melts it. O! What fun

It is to be a child today!
   "Thank you!" is all that I can say!

"Thank you, dear God, for trees that stand
   And shine like trees in Fairyland!

Thank you for the blue of the sky!
   Thank you for a cloud going by!"

Dear God, this is my winter prayer—
   "Thank you for snow-flakes, everywhere!"

BY MARY DIXON THAYER

A WISH

O! I often wish
  That I really could
Always only do
  As you wish I would!

O! I wish that I
  Loved you, God, the way
You ought to be loved!
  I will try today.

Teach Me How to Pray!

AFTERWARDS

When the "Our Father" I have said,
    And mother tucks me into bed,
  And kisses me, and calls "Goodnight,
    God bless you!" and turns out the light—

Why, then I lie awake and say
    Another prayer a diff'rent way.
  I talk to God, and angels keep
    Their wings around me till I sleep.

I talk to God and tell him things
    All in between the angels' wings,
  And God leans down and says "I know.
    I understand. I love you so!"

BY MARY DIXON THAYER

IN THE MORNING

See, God! I make a little prayer
    For you, and through the golden air
Of morning let it fly away
    Across the world, across today,

Across the stars, and on, and on,
    Look, God! It is already gone!
I cannot follow where it goes . . .
    Nobody knows . . . nobody knows

But only you! God, take it please
    Just for a second on your knees
And comfort it—a tiny prayer
    Is so afraid of everywhere!

God, do you think that you could smile
    And play with it a little while?
O! If you only will, I'll try
    To send you others, bye and bye!

TEACH ME HOW TO PRAY!

LOVELY LADY DRESSED IN BLUE

Lovely Lady dressed in blue—
    Teach me how to pray!
God was just your little boy,
    Tell me what to say!

Did you lift him up sometimes,
    Gently on your knee?
Did you sing to him the way
    Mother does to me?

Did you hold his hand at night?
    Did you ever try
Telling stories of the world?
    O! And did he cry?

Do you really think he cares
    If I tell him things—
Little things that happen? And
    Do angels' wings

Lovely Lady dressed in blue—
Teach me how to pray!

Teach Me How to Pray!

Make a noise? And can he hear
    Me if I speak low?
  Does he understand me now?
    Tell me—for you know!

Lovely Lady dressed in blue,
    Teach me how to pray!
  God was just your little boy,
    And you know the way.

BY MARY DIXON THAYER

THANKSGIVING

I want to thank you first of all,
    Dear God, for making me,
Because—if I had not been made—
    I don't know *where* I'd be!

And then I want to thank you, God,
    Especially for my mother.
O! I'm glad I have her, God,
    Instead of any other!

And then I want to thank you for
    My father and the boys,
And for my sisters too, and for
    Our house, and for my toys!

And God, I want to thank you for
    The lovely, lovely sky,
And for the clouds that way, way up
    Above the world go by!

Teach Me How to Pray!

And God, I want to thank you for
    The woods in which we play,
And for the stars and moon by night,
    And for the sun by day . . .

And God, I want to thank you for
    The daisy-fields, and hills
Made to coast down in wintertime,
    And have the biggest spills!

And God, I want to thank you for
    All sorts of little things—
Like curly stems of dandelions
    And pebbles, and the wings

Of butterflies, and icicles,
    And leaves, and bugs that pass—
O! And for diamonds that I find
    Each morning in the grass!

BY MARY DIXON THAYER

Dear God, there are a million things
    To thank you for, I know!
I haven't thought of half of them—
    For instance, there is snow . . .

But God, I don't believe I can
    Remember all that I
Have got to thank you for, and so
    I don't believe I'll try.

But God—you know the way I feel—
    I mean I love you, and
O! Thank you just for everything!
    There! *Now* you understand!

Teach Me How to Pray!

DO YOU REALLY?

God, when I have been very bad—
    Then have I really made you sad?
  And do you really, *truly* care
    What I do always, everywhere?

O yes! I know you do, for I
    Know that you came on earth to try
  To teach us how to work and play
    And how to never disobey;

And if you had not cared for me
    You would not have come down to be
  A child in the world, and die.
    You would have stayed up in the sky!

by Mary Dixon Thayer

FINDING YOU

Dear God, I wish I could have been
    Among those girls and boys
  You called to come and talk to you,
    And who left all their toys,

And ran and climbed up on your knee,
    And held your hand, and sat
  Around you, learning lovely things—
    I *wish* I had done that!

But God, I know that even now
    I can get close to you.
  I know you still love children—yes
    Indeed! I know you do!

And so I often slip away
    Into the church, and kneel
  Down at the altar where you are,
    And tell you all I feel.

Teach Me How to Pray!

I cannot see your face, and yet
    I know that you are there.
I know I'm just as close to you
    As all those children were!

AT PLAY

Often, dear God, when I'm at play
    I think of you, and then I say

"I love you, God!" It only takes
    A second—but it always makes

Me happier to whisper this.
    It's just as if I ran to kiss

You in between our games, and see
    That you are smiling down at me.

BY MARY DIXON THAYER

AN INVITATION

I can't think why you love me, God!
    And yet I know you do!
I know you want me, when I die,
    To come and live with you!

WISHING

Sometimes I really almost hear
    My guardian angel's wings,
And sometimes, God, you come so
        near—
    So near—and whisper things!

I can't quite see you, but I know
    When you lean over me—
O! Then I wish I were as good
    As I should really be!

Teach Me How to Pray!

FIRST COMMUNION

It's almost time! Dear God, I kneel
   And wait for you to come! I feel
   A tiny bit afraid—but O!
   I love you, and of course you know
   I do, and yet you like to hear
   Me say how much when you are near.

Dear God, I love you more than I
   Can tell—but O! Before I die—
   I want to love you more than now!
   So, won't you come and show me how?

BY MARY DIXON THAYER

AFTER COMMUNION

Dear God, dear God, you came to me!
   How glad I am! And yet I see
      I am not what I ought to be.

Here is my heart! It's small, but I
   Have filled it up with love. I'll try
      To keep it that way till I die.

KNOWING

I know wherever I may be
    That God is looking down at me.

I know he made the earth and sky,
    And that the stars come spinning by

Like whirling tops! God makes them go
    Like that! But then I also know

That really nothing is too small
    For God to love. I know that all

The flowers on the hills are dear
    To him as stars, and that down here

Upon the world if I am bad—
    Why! Even I can make God sad!

*I know wherever I may be
That God is looking down at me.*

TEACH ME HOW TO PRAY!

LEARNING

When you were little, God, I know
    You never, never did
What wasn't nice, or anything
    Your mother might forbid.

When you were little, God, I know
    You didn't hide or cry
When bedtime came—and O! I know
    You *never* told a lie!

When you were little, God, I know
    If other little boys
Arrived to play and took away
    Or broke your favorite toys—

You didn't call them names and wish
    They hadn't come at all.
  O! Won't you teach me how to be
    Like you when you were small?

BY MARY DIXON THAYER

BEING TAUGHT

Dear God, I want to always do
    The very best I can
To please you while I am a child,
    And when I am a man.

And though I love you lots today,
    I want to love you more
Tomorrow than today or than
    I ever have before!

HOPES

I hope, dear God, that all I say,
    And do, and think, at work or play,
    Will bring me close to you each day.

O God! I want to get as near
    To you as I can get, down here!

TEACH ME HOW TO PRAY!

PERHAPS HE WON'T

People in church walk quietly,
    And sometimes shake their heads at me
    Very—O! very solemnly!

Of course I know that God is there,
    And that I mustn't talk or stare
    Or laugh or wiggle during prayer.

But yet I know God used to be
    A little child himself, and he
    Won't mind if I am fidgety

In church, perhaps, if only I
    Say all my prayers, and really try
    To be a saint before I die.

by Mary Dixon Thayer

GIVING BACK

I have so many lovely things
    That seem to be my own,
But it was you who gave them all,
    Dear God, and when I'm grown

Please show me how to give them back
    In other ways to you—
Please show me how to give you all
    I have in all I do.

O DO!

Show me how to begin
    To work for you, dear God!
Show me how to keep in
    The little path you trod!

Teach Me How to Pray!

I KNOW

Dear God, I know, although I'm small,
    That everything I do—
Yes—even everything I think—
    Matters a lot to you!

I know, although I am so small,
    That I am just as dear
To you as bigger people are,
    And can come just as near.

O God! Why do you love me so?
    There is no reason why . . .
O please! I want to love you more
    Each day until I die.

BY MARY DIXON THAYER

PLANS

When I grow up I want to be
    A saint because I know, you see,
That that will please you, God,
    more than
    If I am just a famous man.

(Of course I may be famous too—
    I really don't know *what* I'll do . . .)
But God, whatever I decide,
    Please keep me always at your side!

THE THING TO DO

To please you, God, I know that I
    Need not do anything but try
To be as good as I can be
    Because you lived and died for me.

Teach Me How to Pray!

I LOVE YOU

I love you God! Please help me to
    Remember always that I do!

Please make my life into a song
    That sings *"I love you"* all day long!

I love you, God! How can I say
    The same thing in a different way?

But then I know you do not mind
    Although I cannot seem to find

New words to put into a prayer—
    I love you, God! And everywhere

I go, and in all that I do
    I send my love, dear God, to you!

BY MARY DIXON THAYER

WHEN YOU WERE LITTLE

When you were just a little boy,
    Dear God, I know that you
  Obeyed your parents and did not
    Say anything untrue.

When you were just a little boy,
    Dear God, I think, maybe,
  Your mother scolded you sometimes
    The way mine does with me?

And yet I know that you, dear God,
    Did not deserve it when
  This happened, but you never cried,
    Or answered her back then.

O God! I want to be the sort
    Of child you were—I'll try
  To do as I am told, and not
    To answer back, or cry.

Teach Me How to Pray!

JUST THINK

I'm glad, dear God, that when you came
    Down on the world to die,
  You were a little child at first—
    As small and young as I!

Just think! You were a child so that
    All other children could
  Remember what you did, and learn
    From you how to be good!

Just think! You might have floated down
    From heaven on a star!
  You might have been a king the way
    In heaven, now, you are!

Just think! You might have come to us
    Already tall and old—
  You might have been so strict, and
    made
    Us do as we were told!

BY MARY DIXON THAYER

Just think! And yet, instead, you came
    Down as a child and played
With other children, and you had
    A mother you obeyed.

Thank you, dear God! For now I know
    You understand the way
It feels to be a child and have
    Big people to obey.

Teach Me How to Pray!

WHY DO YOU CARE?

Dear God, why do you care so much
    If I am good or bad?
Why do you ever let me make
    You sorry, God, or glad?

If I were you it seems to me
    I wouldn't mind at all
What children do because, you see,
    We really are so small.

But God, I know that what I do
    And think and everything
Is just as serious to you
    As if I were a king!

So please don't let me act as if
    I thought you didn't care—
I know you care—that's why I hope
    That you will hear this prayer!

*Dear God, why do you care so much
If I am good or bad?*

Teach Me How to Pray!

FORGIVE ME

Dear God, sometimes I feel so small,
    And you seem so far off and all!
    Sometimes I say into a mirror,
    "Why can't I do as I want here!"
And sometimes when I kneel to pray,
    My mind is not on what I say.
    Dear God! Forgive me when I do
    And say such selfish things to you.

THE ANSWER

Why do you hide from us, dear God?
    I often wish that I
    Could see you now, and did not have
    To wait until I die!
  But O! I know the reason that
    You hide from us is clear—
    You are too beautiful, dear God,
    For us to see you here.

BY Mary Dixon Thayer

OF COURSE

Dear God, I know you used to be
   A little child on earth like me.

When I am naughty I will try
   To think of you, and not to cry.

And when I want to disobey
   I'll run to you instead, and pray.

Now that I know you used to be
   A little child on earth—like me—

I know you must have understood
   How hard it is to be so good!

Teach Me How to Pray!

PERHAPS . . .

Dear God, I wonder, when you climbed
    The hill of Calvary—
Where were the children that you used
    To take upon your knee?

Where were they? In among the crowd?
    And did they, too, not care
What happened to you, God,
    dear God,
    But only came to stare?

Where were the children that you loved?
    They do not seem to be
Around as you begin to climb
    The hill of Calvary!

O God I wish that I had been
    A child that day! I might
Have done some little thing for you
    To make the cross more light!

BY MARY DIXON THAYER

I might have given you a glass
    Of water on the way—
  I might have whispered, as you passed,
    "I love you so today!"

I might have done this—and yet—O!
    Perhaps I would have hid
  Among the people and done just
    What other children did?

THINKING

God, when I do not think of you—
    When I forget to pray—
    I cannot tell if I am near
    To you or far away.
  O God! Please let me always see
    How far I am from you!
    Please show me what I ought to be,
    And what I ought to do!

Teach Me How to Pray!

FORGETTING

When you are small—like me—it is
    So very easy to
  Forget your prayers, or say them
    Without thinking—when you do!

The world is such a great big place
    To be in when you're small,
  And everything that's in it is
    So wonderful, and all!

Sometimes, dear God, I do not think
    Of you all through the day,
  I only think what fun it is
    To be a child and play!

I only think what fun it is
    To be a child and know
  All sorts of lovely things (like where
    The yellow violets grow,

BY MARY DIXON THAYER

And bluebells, and those little, sad
    White flowers that I love—
  Or where a robin builds his nest—
    Or maybe it's a dove . . .)

I know all sorts of things like that,
    So many, many things—
Why, only just today I found
    A bug with spotted wings!

But God, I know you made the world,
    And all that's in it, and
How I forget you ever, I
    Just *cannot* understand!

Teach Me How to Pray!

MESSAGES

How can I love you more, dear God?
    I really do not know!
  And yet I want to love you more!
    O please—do come and show

Me how! I want to love you, God,
    So much that everything
  Will speak to me of you—so much
    That all the birds will sing

Of you, and all the flowers of
    The world will look at me
  And nod "We love him too!" And trees
    Say softly "So do we . . ."

Dear God! Please let me love you so
    That even little things—
  Like leaves, and grass and butterflies
    With rainbow colored wings,

BY MARY DIXON THAYER

And drops of rain, and little fires
    Of dew upon the grass,
And little fists of baby ferns,
    And little winds that pass

Will tell me lovely secrets, God,
    And speak to me of you.
O! If I listen, I will learn
    So much! But it is true

I sometimes do not listen, and
    I simply go along
And do not ask about you, God,
    And I know that is wrong.

For if I really love you—why!
    The whole wide world will bring
Me messages from you—you'll write
    Me notes on everything!

Teach Me How to Pray!

PLEASE!

God, please make me love you more
   Than I ever have before!

I know that you once used to be
   Just a little child like me—

I know you once came all the way
   Down from heaven, Christmas Day,

Just to show you love us so.
   O yes, dear God, I know, I know.

And so I want to love you more
   Than I ever have before.

BY MARY DIXON THAYER

WORDS

The whole world speaks of you,
    dear God!
  The clouds up in the sky
Tell me about you as they pass,
  And breezes going by

Whisper "Yes—he sent me." And
    The grasses softly say
"We know him too!" And all the trees
    Stand still, and try to pray.

The whole world speaks of you! The sun,
    As it comes up, calls out
"O! See how beautiful I am!
    He made me!" And the shout

Goes all around the world, dear God—
    "He made me—see! O see!"
And in the night-time all the stars
    Keep saying it to me.

Teach Me How to Pray!

Yes! Everywhere I go, dear God,
    And everywhere I look,
  Things speak to me of you, and tell
    Me more than any book.

O God! I've learned such lovely things
    About you from a rose!
  And O! I know that you have taught
    A lily how to close!

I know that you have painted all
    The flowers on the hills—
  And so I think of you, of you—
    When I see daffodils!

*O God! I've learned such lovely things
About you from a rose!*

THE LONELY FEELING

I am so lonely, God, for you
    Sometimes! It seems to me
    You are so far away, and O!
    I wish that I could see
    You now, and hold your hand, and look
    Up in your face, and smile—
    I wish that I could hear you talk,
    Dear God, once in a while!

But after all I know, of course
    That when a child dies
    He finds himself right at the door
    Of your house—Paradise!
    And you will say "Come in! Come in!
    What are you waiting for?
    My child, I love you—and you won't
    Be lonely any more."

BY MARY DIXON THAYER

COMING BACK

Sometimes, dear God, when I've been
  bad,
    I am afraid to pray—
  I feel as if you were so sad
    I'd better stay away.

I feel as if you couldn't want
    Me ever close to you—
  I feel as if you never could
    Forgive the things I do.

But O! I know you said that if
    We really, truly try
  Not to be bad again, you will
    Forgive us, and so I

Come back to you each time and say
    "Dear God! Look what I did!
  I'm sorry God. Please help me to
    Not do what you forbid."

THE MAIN THING

O! People sometimes use such long
    Words when they talk of you,
  I don't know what they mean, dear
    God,
    Although big people do.

But then of course the thing that I
    Need most of all to know
  Is that you came down on the world
    To live a while ago,

And you did this because you love
    Us so, and wish that we
  Would learn how to be good the way
    We really ought to be.

BY MARY DIXON THAYER

HOW KIND!

How kind of you, dear God, to say,
    "Don't make those children go
        away!"
  How kind of you to make us feel
    You really like it when we kneel
Close, close to you! So every day
    I try to go to church and pray!

I know that you are everywhere,
    Dear God, but you are closer there.
When you were in the world you said
    "This is my Body," of the bread.
It's hard to understand, but you
    Would never say what isn't true!

Teach Me How to Pray!

I THINK

Dear God, you are so very kind
    I think you really do not mind
    Although I cannot always pray
    To you in the most solemn way.

I think you really like to hear
    The little things that happen here,
    And so I tell you everything,
    And you are always listening.

I often ask you please to make
    Me much, much better when I wake,
    And then I ask you please to keep
    Your arms around me while I sleep,

Because I know I'm very small
    Compared to angels, saints and all—
    But then I know you used to say
    "Let all the little children stay

Close, close to me!" You did not scold
    "I'll love them later when they're
        old!"
    O no! You said "Come close to me!"
And that is where I want to be!

IF I SHOULD DIE

If I should die today, dear God,
    I don't believe I'd mind.
I know you love me very much
    And that you're very kind.

I know that if I have been good
    There is no reason why
I shouldn't see you right away,
    Dear God, if I should die.

Teach Me How to Pray!

SOMETIMES

Sometimes it is so easy to
    Just kneel right down and pray,
  Or do it standing up, or while
    I am at school, or play.

But other times, dear God, you know
    It's very hard indeed—
  My head gets full of lots of things
    It really doesn't need.

And when I try to think of you,
    And when I try to pray,
  Why! then I find the thoughts inside
    My head are in the way!

I think of silly little things
    Instead, dear God, of you.
  I think of silly things to say,
    And silly things to do.

BY MARY DIXON THAYER

And O! Although I try and try
    To think of what I should,
  The thoughts inside my head jump up
    And say "I *won't* be good!"

But even if they will not all
    Behave, you are so kind
That if I'm sorry, God, dear God,
    Perhaps you do not mind?

FOR YOU

I do not only pray, dear God,
    When I am on my knees,
    But while I work and while I play—
    Yes, all day long! O please—
I want to love you more and more,
    So please help me to do
    My best in all I try today
    For you have asked me to.

Teach Me How to Pray!

LOVING

I love so many people, God!
    In fact I think that I
Love everybody in the world!
    And O! I often try

To make them love me too. I like
    To have them smile at me,
And say, "What a nice child that is!
    Just lovely, isn't she?"

But God, I know I shouldn't care
    So much what people say,
For sometimes I am bad although
    I do not look that way.

Dear God, I know you want me to
    Love people, but I know
I ought to love you most of all
    Of course, dear God, and so

BY MARY DIXON THAYER

When I love anybody I
    Will bring them right to you
And say "Look, God! This is my
    friend!
    Please keep our friendship true!"

A THOUGHT

All that I do—no matter what—
    If it is done for love
Will be a sort of prayer of thanks
    To you, dear God, above!

TEACH ME HOW TO PRAY!

THE STAIRS

I like to think the days are steps
    On which you've set my feet,
And I must climb them one by one,
    Dear God, until we meet.

I like to think the days are steps
  On which you've set my feet.

Teach Me How to Pray!

AT NIGHT

Help me, dear God, to live the way
  You want me to live day by day.

O! Show me how to please you best
  When I'm at work, or play, or rest!

And may I often think of you,
  And never say what isn't true,

And never do what isn't right—
  I think that's all, dear God,
    Goodnight!

BY MARY DIXON THAYER

TO THE BLESSED MOTHER

Mother, I want to always be
    Your child. Will you take care of
        me?
    When God was just a little boy
    I know he gave you lots of joy;
    And though his death then made
        you sad
    I know that now he makes you glad.

And I believe if a child dies
    That, when he gets to Paradise,
    If you'll just touch God's hand and
        say
    "O *please* don't send that child
        away!"
    God will say softly, "Mother dear,
    You can have all you ask for here!"

Teach Me How to Pray!

HOW NICE!

How nice it is, dear God, to know
    That you make all the flowers
        grow!
  How nice it is to stop and think
    You make the water which I drink!

How nice it is to know that you
    Painted the sky that lovely blue!
How nice it is to know you fill
    The night with stars and always
        will!

But O! How nice to know you made
    Me, too! Sometimes I am afraid
I do not thank you as I should—
    You are so wise, dear God, and
        good!

BY MARY DIXON THAYER

WHEN I'M OLD

Dear God, I hope that when I'm old
    I can look back and say
  "I tried to love you better and
    To love you more each day."

And O! I hope that when I'm old
    I can give you my hand,
  And whisper "Ready, God!" and that
    You'll smile, and understand.

TEACH ME HOW TO PRAY!

THOUGHTS

I want to think of you, dear God,
    A million times a day—
  At home, and when I am at school,
    And when I am at play!

No matter who is by, nor where
    I am, nor what I do,
  I know that I can always send
    A thought, dear God, to you!

by Mary Dixon Thayer

IF . . .

I will not keep my love for you
    Locked up inside my heart.
  I will not hide it there, dear God,
    From all the world apart!

O no! I want to love you so
    That this heart never will
Be able to hold all my love,
    And then it soon must spill

Into the hearts of everyone
    I meet, and O! I know
That if I really love you, God,
    It's sure to happen so!

Teach Me How to Pray!

NOW

Of course it will be easy, God,
   To love you when I see
   You face to face in heaven and
   You put your arms 'round me!
It will be easy then, of course,
   To love you as I should—
   But O! while I can't see you, it
   Is harder to be good!
Dear God, you know how hard it is
   Because you tried it too—
   You came down on the world to teach
   Us what we ought to do.
You know it's hard to act as if
   I saw you every day,
   And yet, dear God, I know that you
   Are near me when I pray.
I know that every single time
   I think of you, you lean
   Down out of Paradise to me
   And nothing comes between!

BY MARY DIXON THAYER

SOME CHILDREN

Some children have so little, God,
    Compared with me! And they
Are bad, sometimes, but then no one
    Has taught them how to pray.

When I am bad it is so much,
    Much worse because I take
All that you give me, and I know
    That when I'm bad I make

You sad, dear God, and yet I go
    And do wrong just the same—
O yes! Sometimes I even put
    On someone else the blame!

O! Show me how to use the things
    You give, so you won't be
Too sorry that you gave them (out
    Of all the world) to me!

Teach Me How to Pray!

WHAT WILL I DO!

When I see you at last, dear God,
    I wonder what you'll say?
I wonder if I'll feel ashamed
    And want to run away?

I wonder, when I kneel, at last,
    And look into your eyes,
And all the angels bow their heads
    Up there in Paradise . . .

I wonder . . . will I feel ashamed
    Because I didn't do
All that I might have done, dear God,
    Down in the world, for you?

And even if you smile and take
    My hand, dear God, will I
Be happy? Won't I want to hide
    Away somewhere—and cry?

BY MARY DIXON THAYER

TO THINK!

To think you care, dear God, for me
    Who really am so small!
  To think that anything I do
    Means much to you at all!

Why! All the angels, looking on,
    Must feel sad when they see
How little I love you compared
    With how much you love me!

O! Show me how to love you more!
    I want to love you, God!
I want to follow, through the world,
    The same path that you trod!

Teach Me How to Pray!

WHAT I DO KNOW

I know I'll never understand
    (At least not till I die)
  A lot of things, dear God, and yet
    My head keeps asking "Why?"

Why do some people cry and wish
    They never had been made?
  Why are some people sick, dear God,
    And hungry and afraid?

My head keeps asking "Why? Why? Why?"
    And yet, I understand
  That I am much too little to
    Know all that you have planned.

And after all, dear God, I know
    When you were here you cried—
  Like us—and you were poor, and you
    Were laughed at, and you died!

*Why are some people sick, dear God,
And hungry and afraid?*

TEACH ME HOW TO PRAY!

PRESENTS

I think, dear God, the nicest prayer
   Is thinking of you, everywhere!

All day long my heart keeps saying
   "For you, God!" And that is praying.

So, out of all I think and do
   I can make presents, God, for you.

O! I will always try to give
   You lots of presents while I live!

BY MARY DIXON THAYER

THE FIRST PRESENT

All by myself I never can
    Do anything that's fine.
  But when you help me, God, then I
    Can give you all that's mine.

And so I give you everything
    I have, and myself too,
  And you can do with me, dear God,
    Just as you want to do!

Teach Me How to Pray!

SOME DAYS

Some days, dear God, you seem so near
    I really almost feel
  You right beside me all the time,
    And when at night I kneel

To say my prayers it seems as if
    I really ought to see
  You standing there beside my bed,
    Or leaning over me!

But other times, dear God, you seem
    So far—so very far!
  And then I wonder if you hear
    My prayers, and where you are?

And O! Then it is hard, you know,
    To pray the way I should—
  When you seem far away and I
    Don't feel like being good!

BY MARY DIXON THAYER

Dear God, remind me every prayer
    I ever say, you hear.
Remind me when you seem far off,
    You *really* are quite near.

SO MUCH!

You love each one of us, dear God.
    Such a great deal, I know—
    Such a great deal, you could not love
    Us more—and even though
    I were the only child upon
    The world, dear God, you would
    Have died for me—just me—to teach
    Just me how to be good!

THE MISTAKE

Though people sometimes look at me
    And say nice things, and smile,
I know I'm not as good as I
    May seem once in a while.

I know, dear God, that lots of times
    I'm really very bad.
  O! Lots of times, dear God, I know
    I make you very sad!

Then why, I wonder, am I glad
    When people smile at me
And think that I am nicer than
    I am? I ought to be

Ashamed, I ought to tell them that
    There's surely some mistake—
And yet I don't! O no! I feel
    Quite proud! Dear God, please
    make

by Mary Dixon Thayer

Me really good! I do not want
    To only be a sham.
  Please make me good—or anyway
    Much better than I am!

COMFORT

I am so very little, God!
    What can you do with me?
  I don't see how what is so small
    Of any use can be!

O! But I know you do not care
    If I am big or small—
  You only ask me for my heart,
    Dear God, my heart—that's all!

Teach Me How to Pray!

TRYING

Dear God, I know that when I say
    My prayers you always lean
Down out of heaven, and you know
    Exactly what I mean.

O yes, dear God! I know you hear
    All that I want to say—
Yes, even when the words get mixed
    In a most awful way!

Yes! Even when I think of lots
    Of silly little things
Instead of only you, or saints,
    Or angels with white wings—

Yes! Even then you always will
    Forgive me, God, if I
Kneel down and say "I will be
    good" . . .
    And really, truly try!

BY MARY DIXON THAYER

GROWING

It seems to me I really *don't*
    Grow better day by day—
I'm naughty lots of times, dear God,
    In every sort of way!

And yet I think I really ought
    To be quite good by now,
For I am nearly ten, and you
    Have told, and told, me how!

O! But I know I am not good
    The way I ought to be,
In spite of all that you have done
    Dear God, dear God, for me!

You won't get tired—will you, God—
    Of helping me? For I
Do want to please you and be good—
    And O! I really try!

Teach Me How to Pray!

THE DIFFERENCE

I know the world would not be half
    As lovely, God, if you
Had never come to live on it,
    And tell us what is true.

Of course, even before you came,
    The flowers used to grow,
And there were stars, and birds, and trees,
    And clouds, and wind and snow.

(Perhaps there are some people yet
    Who think—before you came—
That everything here in the world
    Was just about the same)

O! But I know that all the world
    Is different, dear God,
Since you came down to tell us that
    You love us—since you trod

BY MARY DIXON THAYER

The world I'm very sure that all
    The trees and flowers now
Are much, much prettier, dear God,
    And when the big trees bow

Their heads, and when the faces of
    The little stars look out,
Or when the sun is shining and
    The birds sing all about . . .

O! Everything is lovelier
    Because you used to be
A child here in the world, dear God—
    A little child   like me!

Teach Me How to Pray!

IF ONLY

I wish I'd been a child, dear God,
    When you were little too!
  O! Think of all the lovely things
    We would have thought to do!

Perhaps I would have lived across
    The street, and every day
  Perhaps you would have asked me to
    Come over, God, and play?

Perhaps you would have taught me how
    To saw up wood or clean
  The shop or build a little house?—
    What fun *that* would have been!

And then perhaps when we had worked
    At that for quite a while,
  Your mother would have fixed our lunch
    And kissed us with a smile!

I wish I'd been a child, dear God,
  When you were little too!

Teach Me How to Pray!

O! If I'd only been a child
    When you were little too!
Just *think*, dear God, of all the things
    We would have thought to do!

A GIFT

Take all of me today, dear God!
    I want to give you all
I think and do and say and am,
    From morning till nightfall!

I want to live for you today!
    I want to try and fill
The minutes up with love for you—
    And O! I hope I will!

BY MARY DIXON THAYER

PEOPLE

The loveliest people are always
    The people who keep just as near
    To you, dear God, as they can—and so
    Of course it is quite, quite clear
    That the reason I love these people
    (And everyone knows it is true)
    Is that all these people are lovely
    Because they're in love with you!

Teach Me How to Pray!

WAKING UP

As soon as I wake up, I say
  "Please help me, God, to live today
  For you—just you!" And then I pray
  A little while in my own way.

And when I get up out of bed
  Such lovely thoughts are in my head!
  I feel all sort of comforted!
  I *know* I'll see you when I'm dead!

BY MARY DIXON THAYER

IF I WERE YOU

Yes, dear God! I know you love me!
    And yet I can't see why!
It seems to me if I were you
    I wouldn't even try.

It seems to me if I were you
    I'd simply say "O well,
Why should I bother what they do
    Down on the world?" I'd tell

One of the angels please to give
    The world a push, and it
Would roll away, away, away . . .
    (I wouldn't care a bit!)

O! But I'm glad, dear God, that you
    Are not as I would be
If I were you—you are so good,
    So kind and good to me!

A GOOD WAY

Let's see, dear God, I want to tell
    You in a brand new way
"I love you!" But I cannot think
    Of anything to say.

I know, dear God! I'll run and do
    Something for someone, and
Then when you see me doing it
    Of course you'll understand!

BY MARY DIXON THAYER

THE VERY TIME

I used to think, if I'd been bad,
    I'd better stay away
From you, dear God, I used to think
    I might as well not pray.

I used to think, if I'd been bad,
    You wouldn't want me to—
And so I didn't pray, but now
    Of course I always do.

Now when I have been bad, dear God,
    I always quickly fall
Down on my knees for then—O then
    I need you most of all!

Teach Me How to Pray!

MAYBE

Sometimes, when I kneel down to pray,
   I can't think of a thing to say,
   And God seems—O! So far away!

And then I wish that I could see
   Him just as well as he sees me—
   O! Think how lovely that would be!

But if I'm good, and if I grow
   Up loving him, I will, I know,
   At last go where the angels go.

Then I will run to God, and he
   Will take me up upon his knee
   (At least I think he will . . . maybe)

I really think he will be glad
   To have me if I've not been bad
   Here on the world and made him sad.

So I will sit there on God's knee,
   And he will keep his arms 'round me—
  (At least I *think* he will . . .
      maybe . . .)

A PUZZLE

How can I really, truly want
    To please you, and yet be
As naughty as I am sometimes?
    O God, I do not see!

ANGELS

Dear God, I'm sure the angels keep
   Their arms around me when I sleep!

For sometimes, when I wake at night—
   Yes, when my eyes are still shut
      tight—

I hear all sorts of little things
   That sound just like an angel's wings!

It wouldn't be a great surprise
   If, when I opened up my eyes

I saw an angel by the bed
   And touched the halo 'round his head!

BY MARY DIXON THAYER

NOT UNLESS . . .

Dear God I wish—I wish I could
   Get suddenly so good, so good
   That even all the saints would be
   Astonished when they looked at me!

But O! I know—O yes, I know
   There is no use in wishing so
   Unless I try, day after day
   To do what's right in every way.

Then maybe, if I try and try,
   Maybe at last—before I die—
   I will be nearly what I should?
   O God, I wish—I *wish* I would!

Teach Me How to Pray!

TAKE ALL OF ME

Each morning when I wake I say
  "Take all of me, dear God, today!"

I give you all I am, although
  That isn't much, dear God, I know—

But still I say "Take all of me!"
  I have no more to give, you see.

EXCUSES

O God, why am I ever bad
  When being so makes you so sad?

And O! Why don't I always do
  The things that you have told me to?

Dear God, dear God, I'm very small—
  But that is no excuse at all.

BY MARY DIXON THAYER

WAITING

O! If I could be sure
    Each day I love you more
  Than any other day
    That's ever been before!

O! If I could be sure
    Each day I come more near
  To you, dear God, than I
    Have ever come down here!

O! If only I could
    Be sure, quite sure that I
  Will give you all you want
    From me before I die!

O God, I wish I knew
    If you are pleased with me?
  The only thing to do
    Is just to wait and see.

Teach Me How to Pray!

TELL ME WHAT?

I want to do so much for you,
    Dear God, I want to be
  One of the people that you choose
    To do your work. Ask me!

O! Please don't ever be afraid,
    Dear God, to ask me to
  Do what is hard, for that is just
    What I would *like* to do!

BY MARY DIXON THAYER

REMIND ME

Dear God, dear God, if ever I
    Forget you here, before I die—

O! Please remind me right away
    So that I will kneel down and say

"Forgive me, God! I love you yet!"
    (But O! I hope I *won't* forget).

Teach Me How to Pray!

DIFFERENT WAYS

Dear God, I try to tell you
    Through all the busy day
"I love you!" And to say it
    In every sort of way.

I say it in the morning
    By jumping out of bed
Just when I ought to do it
    You know, dear God, instead

Of lying there and thinking
    How comfy beds can be—
For that would not be loving
    You, God—but loving me!

And then I say "I love you!"
    By washing as I should,
And all day long I say it
    By trying to be good . . .

... *instead*
Of lying there and thinking
How comfy beds can be—

Teach Me How to Pray!

"I love you, God! I love you!"
    There are as many ways
Of saying that I love you
    As there are nights and days!

BY MARY DIXON THAYER

YOUR FRIENDS

Because I love you, God, I love
    The saints—for what are they
But people who have loved you in
    A very special way.

Of course I love your friends, dear God,
    And I would like to know
Them very, very well, because—
    Because I love *you* so!

Teach Me How to Pray!

WHAT TO DO

When any thought that isn't good
    Gets in my head, I say
A little prayer, and then that thought
    Turns 'round and runs away!

TRADING

Dear God, I know that if I loved
    You very much—then I
Would do more for you than I do—
    Or anyway, I'd try!

O! Teach me how to love you more,
    Dear God, I want to give
You all my life, so please—O please
    Do show me how to live!

BY MARY DIXON THAYER

THE WRONG IDEA

Sometimes I really feel as if
    I really was quite good!
  Sometimes I really feel as if
    I did all that I should!

O! Why is it so easy, God,
    Sometimes, for me to make
Myself believe that I am good
    When this is a mistake?

Teach Me How to Pray!

HOW TO TURN FUN INTO PRAYERS

You know I try, dear God, to give
    You presents every day—
Not only when I am at school,
    But when I am at play.

Not only when I'm doing things
    That I have got to do,
But when I'm having fun—O! Then
    I give you presents too!

For when I'm having fun, I say
    "O thanks, dear God!" You see,
That turns the fun into a prayer
    For you, dear God, from me.

BY MARY DIXON THAYER

FOLLOW THE LEADER

Take me, God, and make me
    What I ought to be!
  O! I want to please you!
    But I cannot see

Always how to do it
    In the nicest way
  'Till you come and tell me—
    So I kneel and say

"Show me how to please you
    More and more, dear God!
  Show me how to follow
    Just where you have trod!"

Teach Me How to Pray!

SUPPOSE . . .

Suppose, dear God, in spite of all
    These prayers I really am
Not getting better? O! Suppose
    I'm nothing but a sham?

Dear God, I know that you are sad
    If anybody prays
And then goes off and doesn't think
    Of you in other ways.

I know, dear God, that if I say
    "I love you!" and then go
And do what isn't right—then you
    Are sad, *so* sad, I know!

O! Teach me how to live for you
    Each minute of the day!
Not only when I kneel and bow
    My head, dear God, and pray!

THE SUREST WAY

Help me, dear God, to follow in
    Your footsteps everyday!
  Yes, even when they seem to me
    To lead a hilly way!

O! Do not ever let me try
    A shorter cut, dear God!
  The surest way to find you is
    Along the path you trod.

REMEMBERING

How nice it was of you to be
    A little child, dear God!
  I love to think my feet are on
    The same world that you trod!